THE

Anthology

OF WRITING AND ARTWORK
BY EAST BAY TEENAGERS

Volume One – Spring 2010

FOUNDERS, EDITORS, AND PUBLISHERS: Theo Olesen and Ian Hoffman
DESIGNER AND TYPE ILLUSTRATOR: Theo Olesen
ASSISTANT COPYEDITOR: Daniel Remler
THANKS to Jenna Archer, Richard Raya, Eugenio Geiken, Lias Djili, Dylan
Lopez, Zachary Wilson, Mary Pinto, Pauline Velez, Hesham Muthana,
Arsia Sarlak, Kyle Filippelli, Benjamin Sanoff, Doug Dohrer, Kerry Erspamer,
Karla Herndon, Philip Halpern, Matthew Carton, Timothy Zolezzi,
Kate Rosen, Carl Rogers, Matthew Meyer, Matthew Bussa, Jonathan Pinto,
Robin Cohen, Paul Leonard-Monrad, Rick Jaffe, Deborah Davis, Clementine
and Joseph Greenberg, Peter Wegner, Robin and Walker Olesen, Carol Hoff-
man, James Matson, and Jim Slemp.
SPECIAL THANKS to Cara Hunt, Gabi and Shira Rothman, Ivy Olesen, and
Lauren and Ella Hoffman.

ANTHOLOGY CONCEPT by Theo Olesen.

First Printing: April 2010

CALLING ALL TEEN WRITERS AND ARTISTS!

To submit your work for publication in this winter's
Anthology, send it to teenswrite2010@gmail.com by
February 15th, 2010.

CONTENTS

WRITING

ARTWORK

INTRODUCTION

Ian Hoffman and Theo Olesen, Editors

"Are you guys actually getting anything *good?*"

A few weeks after we began receiving submissions for The Anthology, we started hearing this question a lot. Truthfully, we were thrilled that kids were sending us anything at all.

We had begun the project assuming that submissions would be hard to come by, that we would have to cajole and coerce our friends into sending us their English papers and notebook doodles. Although we suspected that a vast, untapped pool of incredible teenage art and writing existed in the East Bay, we had no idea how to convince our peers to send their work to us. We anticipated receiving about ten submissions from close friends, adding ten of our own, and making a small book.

Two months later, our minds were blown.

We stared at the screen, slack-jawed, as we scrolled through dozens of submissions. We had received work that encompassed every topic imaginable, from homophobia to yoga to viscous American cheese.

Teenagers from seventeen East Bay high schools and colleges had sent us more than 600 pieces of writing and artwork.

We had not expected this.

As we began to read all the work we had received, we were shocked to discover that most of it – all of it – was much better than we had expected. In fact, most of it was excellent. Our publicity campaign had worked.

We had spent the last month blanketing the East Bay with flyers and advertisements. We had enlisted friends to spread the word at their schools, and we had spent many weekends walking around different neighborhoods, taping up thousands of flyers. We had silkscreened 60 T-shirts and sold out within a week. We hoped our efforts would increase the number of submissions we received, but we never expected to have 600 stories, poems, essays and works of art to choose from.

Selecting pieces for The Anthology was incredibly difficult. Each submission was special, and we wish we could publish everything we received. The 66 pieces that we eventually settled on represent the diversity and originality of teenagers in the East Bay, and each one is a stunning example of the creativity and passion that teens everywhere possess.

Enjoy the daydreams, doodles, and ruminations of teenagers – all of us.

AIMÉE THANATOGENOS REMIXED

Sarah Li

her city reeks of industrialization and hooded sunsets
gas pumps churn blood into the hearts of metal,
and it courses –
courses through cracks in the sidewalk,
through the tips of her polished fingers,
through the holes in her Brand Name Sneakers.
doesn't make much of a difference, she supposes,
the way you can't tell skin from denim.
that's how it is in this city.
she can't say she blames them.
she props her bike up on the hill
and wonders
if she's ever seen a sunset
not framed by lonely hearts and telephone wires.

MAYBE AUTUMN DAYS

Emma Carlblom

Memories
seem so clear.
So blurred
In time
In retelling and exaggeration
I wonder what the ingredients of life really are
Behind elements and chemicals
Maybe it has something to do with
the feel of autumn days
Cold air pushing against rosy cheeks
Leaves and rain swirling from open skies
Anything can be
What make it

Nick Stinehour

HYPONATRAEMIA

Sarah Li

Three days ago I might've been alive and believed everything you told me. But there is not enough water in the world to keep us all alive, and when you speak, all I hear are bubbles and sea foam. Three days ago I might've been able to understand this Neptunian language of yours, but I am now a fish out of water, and I cannot hear you over the noise of chapped lips and dry lungs and my own desperate pleas.

Won't anybody let me in?

You asked me what had happened, and I told you everything you wanted to hear, but none of it was true: "I was greedy, and I couldn't get enough, and I took you for granted, and I don't know what to do anymore. I'm so lost, and I'm so sorry."

But this is what I really meant: "I'm still greedy and still can't get enough, and I want you, need you, love you, hate you, and I'm just so damned thirsty these days, all right? Please."

But we don't understand each other anymore anyway, and we are never on the same page because paper and books and ink and pen and water do not mix. My words turn soggy and unintelligible, and you never cared to learn how to read anyway.

The sun sits unmoved on the horizon, always shining and exposing everything I never wanted to know. I am reminded that diving into the deep end only means that I'll be hung out to dry when I resurface, that I am only dirty laundry to be aired, that I never belonged in water in the first place.

You were the first to tell me about evolution. "Fish are meant to grow legs, you know? Then they strut around as if they own the world and write about the Meaning of Life, about Existentialism and Nihilism, theology and metaphysics, and all that. They think they've got it all figured out. Rather silly for a bunch of fish, don't you think?" you used to say with a sarcastic laugh as you waved cascades through my hair and I pretended I was paying attention. "And then they get so caught up with themselves they forget that they're really all the same, that they all came from the same place. They forget where they even came from."

I hadn't realized you were referring to me.

Day four and I find myself waist-deep in your waters, starfish tracing lazy circles under my feet and jellyfish pulsating lethargically about my knees. Your water is dirty and brackish, always making me crave more. I try to resist the urgent pull of the tide and the fact that I have not had water for days, so I do the only thing I know: I scream and cry and yell and pretend the world is paying attention, but my voice is loud and hoarse and crass, and you've had enough.

You pull me ten feet underwater and scream, "Who can hear you now?" And for the first time in three days, I do not hear bubbles and sea foam but words, explicit and raw. I am pulled in deeper, and you remind me that there is more to water than a pretty blue surface. But it's too late for that, and the last thing I see before I'm swept away is the pale glow of a light that could've been the sun.

But I have not yet learned the anatomy of an anglerfish.

They say you can only survive three days without water. But it's been four days, and I've had too much.

RAIN

Alison Thvedt

The leftover rain

It plays a honky-tonk step

Dancing on windows

Gemma Searle

THE UNUSUAL CIRCUMSTANCE

Emma Dudley

As far back as I can remember, the only way I ever heard my father describe our family was with the two words "unusual circumstance." As a child I struggled with those words, often tossed into different sentences and lectures, said as an indisputable answer to any questions I might think of now or in the future. I used my dad's words to begin to connect the pieces as best I could.

My mom being in the army, at war, was an unusual circumstance.

My dad not being in the army, at war, was an unusual circumstance.

My brother wanting nothing to do with my dad was an unusual circumstance.

I, myself, was in an unusual circumstance, and there was nothing in the world I could do to change this.

I finally decided that all of these unusual circumstances connected back to war. War was the short but huge word my father spoke of with disgust and dejection, and my brother with admiration and longing. There were only three letters in the word war, but somehow it seemed to have infinite definitions and implications that I would never be able to understand. I viewed all of the arguments between my dad and brother and even the news I heard from the TV as an outsider, not getting involved, just observing as you would some foreign film in a language you can't comprehend.

There were emails. Emails from her, my mother, who I remembered enough for there to be some significance in what I read, but not enough to miss her, exactly. She didn't seem like an actual person, just an object that typed out words for me to look at. Maybe it was just the distance, or maybe the lack of clarity in the memories. The Middle East was too far away for me to understand.

I didn't ask when she was coming home, or when I would see her again. Sometimes I heard my dad murmuring about the possibility of her never coming back. So I distanced myself further from her.

I did sometimes ask my brother about my dad, however. One night I went into his room and sat down on his bed.

"Zack, why doesn't Dad like to read the letters?"

Zack slowly capped a small bottle and shoved it out of my sight into a drawer.

"Prob'ly wishes he was the one getting the glory," he said.

"You mean he's jealous of Mom?"

"Sure. He doesn't like to be the lowly housekeeper, staying home while Mom takes care of business out there." Zack's face was red.

"Then why didn't he go to war, too?"

Zack smashed his index finger against his lips. "'Cuz he's a coward. But don't tell him I said that!" He spoke around either side of the finger.

"Okay," I said, walking out of the room.

Looking back, I think Zack must have felt as confused and powerless as I did, but just didn't know it.

Another day, when I was older, I asked Zack if he would come with me to play catch. I wanted to try out for the

third grade club team and Zack agreed that I needed the
practice badly. I remember that it was a hot day in early
spring. I put on my poker-pitcher face that Zack had taught
me early in life and fired the ball towards my brother's mitt.

"Nice one," Zack said.

We continued to throw back and forth.

"Zack?"

"Yeah?"

"Is baseball like war?"

Zack frowned out from under the bill of his hat. "Why
do you ask that?"

"Well, is it?"

"I guess."

"How is it like war?"

Zack caught the ball but didn't throw it back. "Well, all
sports are a little like war. Some were originally used to
train people for war."

"Did they use baseball to train for war?"

"I dunno, Gabe. I doubt it. Baseball's a gentleman's
game."

All the way home, I kept repeating what Zack had said
in my head. "Gentleman's game." From what I'd seen in
the movies at that point, it looked like war used to be more
gentlemanly than it was at the present. The opposing forces
would line up, all nice and orderly, and shoot at each other.
There were no people dropping out of trees or firing from
the air. Those old soldiers died with honor, and, it seemed,
stupidity. I didn't get how you could stand there doing nothing, in your line, just waiting to get shot.

Back then there weren't any women in the army, either.
Is that another reason why Dad felt bitter about the war?
Did he think he wasn't honorable, that he wasn't a gentle-
man?

I was beginning to realize that I wanted answers. I wasn't content not to understand anymore. I wanted to be a part of my family and to understand the issues that tore us apart.

So I answered one of the emails.

Well, I didn't answer so much as ask.

My dad and occasionally my brother answered the emails from my mom, but I never had. Somehow it would have felt like intruding. They were never written directly to me, anyway, even though my name was typed at the beginning of each one, along with Zack's and my father's. But the messages were general. The messages did not contain the answers I wanted, not yet.

Dear Mom,

This is Gabe writing. How are you? It's good to hear everything's okay over there. We're glad.

What's it like there? Are people scared of you? Are you scared of people? Do you wear the same uniform every day, or do you have different ones?

Write me back,

Love,

Gabe

P.S. Do you play baseball to train for war?

I was happy with what I had written. I figured it covered my biggest questions. Hopefully she would write back with answers.

So I waited.

And she did answer.

Dear Gabriel,

It is so nice to hear from you. It sounds like you have a lot of ques-

tions. Where I am it's mostly desert. It's not the kind of desert that looks like an ocean, though; it just lasts forever and is a solid tan color with rocks.

Some people are scared of my friends and me, others are angry or sad. I'm scared, but not as much as I was when I first arrived. I've learned to just take every day as it comes and not think too much about anything.

We do have different uniforms for different times. We have combat uniforms, relaxing uniforms, dress uniforms, etc...

We don't have much free time, but sometimes I do throw a ball around with some friends. I hear you're going out for baseball. Good luck – I know you'll do great!

Lots of love,
Mom

I stared at the computer screen for a long, long time.

For the first time, my questions had been answered directly. The letter was short, but that was because nothing had been hidden or dumbed-down for me, it was just straight and to the point. Raw facts had been written for my eyes to scan by this woman I didn't even technically know anymore. Somehow, she seemed to know exactly what I wanted. She seemed to know me better than anyone.

I began to write with an intense hunger for answers clicked onto the computer screen by my mother. She was my idol, the one thing in my life that was steady. She was thousands of miles away, but because of this she never came home smelling and acting funny, like Zack, and she never sat staring at the newspaper with a grimace painted on her face for hours, like Dad.

We began to completely understand and trust each other.

I trusted her to answer every letter...

Dear Gabe,

I'm going to be deployed on a mission soon and won't have Inter-net. I'll try my hardest to write you letters by hand.

Hang in there,

Love,

Mom

At first I was excited. My mom, on a real mission! I was proud of her; I'd seen this in all the movies. I was look-ing forward to seeing exactly how she wrote, what kind of paper she used, what the ink would smell like. I wondered what the word "love" might look like written by hand before her name. I wondered if the L would sweep under the o, v, and e, I wondered if I would feel even more connected to her when I saw those four letters.

Then I was disappointed. Apparently my mother's "hardest" wasn't hard enough.

One day I couldn't stand the waiting any longer. I was staring out the window as the mailman stuffed our mail into the box. Just as soon as the envelopes had left his hand I was sprinting through the door and down the stairs.

"Hey there," the mailman said.

"Hi," I said, throwing the door to the mailbox open and snatching at the letters. Nothing.

I looked up. The mailman was walking down the street to the next house. "Wait!" I yelled, running after him. "Do you know how long a letter from the Middle East would take to get here? To my house?"

The mailman stopped and looked down at me. "Anywhere from a week to a over a month, really. Got somebody over there?"

I nodded. "Well, it's been over a month now."

Pity seeped into the mailman's eyes. "Your dad or brother is probably really busy now, just give it some time. Hang in there." He walked away.

I walked back up to my room.

It had been over a month.

My dad was not over there.

My brother was not over there.

And I was tired of hanging in there.

My father grew silent. When he did speak, it was in deep, scary tones, mostly directed at my brother or me. He was impatient about everything, from getting ready for school to getting to bed on time. But really, it all went back to being impatient about one thing... word from my mother.

They say that if someone loses one sense, another will take over and become stronger for them. In a way, my ears got used to the silence of my house, but my nose opened up to the strong, ever-present stench of my brother. Even when he was acting like himself, there was always a faint, sicken- ingly sweet smell about him. I still didn't know what it was. I only associated it with my brother. It became "his" smell, like other kids might think of their mother's perfume.

One day, my brother, not my dad, arrived to pick me up from school. It was just the end of another fifth grade school day, but my whole body clenched up when I saw his used pickup sagging into a parking space. Zack opened the door and jumped down, weaving towards where I was standing with some other kids in my class. He hadn't shaved in a few days, and there was a big stain on one of the legs of his jeans.

"Who's that?" A boy asked me.

"My brother," I said quietly.

The kids around me grew silent as Zack came to stand

in front of me.

"Come on," he said a little too loudly. "Dad said to pick you up, so here I am."

It struck me that my classmates might find Zack scary. As I looked at his pale, unpredictable blue eyes and his unshaved chin, I realized that *I* was a little scared. I nodded quickly and followed him to the car.

As I passed by, I heard a boy whisper to a girl, "Smells like weed."

I squeezed my eyes shut and took a deep breath.

My brother didn't smell like weed. Weed smelled like my brother.

Finally, we did hear something. Mom was coming home. When we got the letter, my dad grunted. My brother didn't do anything. I cleaned my room.

Now that I think about it, it may have been a good thing that I wasn't able to remember much of anything about my mother. After she first arrived, I only heard her speak a half dozen words over a whole two weeks. Her eyes flickered from glazed to terrified in split seconds. I couldn't technically be disappointed because I had nothing to base the feeling on.

She had a long cut down her cheek. It looked like the stitches had recently come out. I sometimes saw her running a finger over it, tracing its path.

Could this be the same woman who had written those emails? It seemed impossible. The emails were so full of life, overflowing with hope and enthusiasm. It depressed me that remembering those messages brought me more happiness and better memories than seeing her in the flesh at the kitchen table ever did.

My mom went to a class for returned soldiers every Wednesday night. According to Zack, it was really a class for returned soldiers "with issues." It seemed like Zack was disgusted with our mother.

"Do patriots even exist anymore?" I heard him muttering from his bedroom. "How can you come back from all that, with a gash on your face and everything, not even talking? Not even living?"

Maybe he had expected her to come running home wrapped in a huge American flag, screaming praise to our nation at the top of her lungs instead of slouching onto our doorstep, looking troubled. Whatever he had expected, Zack had little tolerance for her.

Zack's reaction was clear and to the point. My father's, on the other hand, was impossible to read. He didn't say much of anything either. It was like he didn't know what to do with himself around my mother. I could see him struggling to come up with conversations that might interest her or trying to decide whether or not to give her a peck on the cheek when he got home from work. Mostly, he just stared at the newspaper.

It seemed like we were all disappearing, bit by bit. Zack back into his room, Dad into his newspaper, Mom into herself. I felt like I was disappearing sometimes, too, I just didn't know where I might be going.

Five days after my mother's return, I woke up in the middle of the night to pee. I walked past my parent's room and saw that the door was wide open. I peeked in. My mother was sitting bolt upright, as far away from my dad's sleeping form as she could manage without falling off the bed. She seemed to be frozen in place, her eyes transfixed on something far, far away. Probably on something all the way back in the desert.

I knew my dad was an extremely deep sleeper, so I walked up to her side. I was a little afraid, but I knew I had to find out what was wrong. I poked her shoulder.

"Mom?" I said.

"Mom?" I repeated. "What's wrong? Did you have a bad dream?"

My mother's head jerked towards me. I jumped back and stifled a shout.

"A bad dream?" she said clearly. I still wasn't used to hearing her voice.

She shook her head and blinked, as if trying to get her thoughts together. "Everything is so muddled up, Gabe. So hard… A bad dream?" She stared at me. Her eyes were the same color as Zack's.

"Um, yeah, did you have a bad dream?" I stammered.

My mother looked away again. She was quiet for a long time. "Yes," she whispered. "Yes, I've had a very bad dream. But not the kind I'll forget when I wake up again. Because I think the dream has bled into my real life, Gabe. And I don't think I'll ever be able to share it with anyone, or get it out of my head again. That woman…" She was crying.

I stared. I had no idea what to say or how to help. She was tracing the cut with her index finger frantically. I tried to imagine what might have happened. Had someone stabbed her? Had something exploded? Had someone exploded near her? It was horrible enough to imagine the possibilities. I realized that these questions couldn't be asked out loud. They couldn't even be put into an email.

She was supposed to make it all better. Her job was to come into my room when I woke up from a nightmare and know exactly how to calm me down and make me feel better.

I decided not to say anything because I knew there was nothing I *could* say. My mother was utterly and completely alone. None of us understood. I took her cold hand in my own. This was what war meant, right here in front of me.

I understood then that I might not ever be able to understand.

My mother got better, little by little. She smiled and talked more often, and seemed able to enjoy things more. Her scar faded with time and laser surgery appointments.

I don't think she ever got back to the person she was when she wrote those letters, though. She never got back to the person she was before she ever left for war.

She came to my middle school graduation. My first junior varsity, and then varsity, baseball games. She hugged me when I got accepted to the University of California, Santa Barbara. She was there for all the important events; at least whatever part of her remained untouched by what she had seen and done.

Zack was not there to see me off to college. He disappeared one night after living with us for seven years since Mom's return. One day the pickup was there, the next it wasn't. It was that gratingly simple. He didn't take his cell phone with him. He left a letter, stuck onto the fridge with a cat-shaped magnet.

Family:
When I was little, I thought things were going to turn out a certain way, exactly how I planned and expected them. Bit by bit, I learned this was far from true. I expected you, Dad, to support Mom and her cause. I expected you, Mom, to support and care about your own cause and country.

Gabe, I expected you to be a little more interesting to live with and maybe have something in common with me. But I guess things really do never turn out as planned.
-Zack

I cried that night. I was eighteen years old, a grown man, but I cried like I had never cried before after reading those words. More than anything, I cried because I had always thought Zack was my connection to the real world, to the big picture. He had explained things to me when I was little, and I had understood that he was always right about things, no matter what.

I never heard from Zack again, but I did see his name in the Army's "deceased" list, printed in the newspaper.

* * *

I look up at the gray plane that will take me where I'm needed. My mother needed me that night. Zack needed me time and time again, but was too afraid to admit it. My father needed me not to be needed, at least in this circumstance.

But circumstances can change. Circumstances can be unusual.

I need to find out what all this was really about. One of my family members survived, but left something back in a place where it could never be retrieved. Another did not survive. Maybe he somehow gained something in the process, accomplished what he needed to. I don't know what I will lose, what I will gain. All I know is that now it's my turn.

I look up at the gray plane and then down at my United States Army uniform. As sharp as those desert-colored pixels must have appeared when they were first printed, they look like a blur to me now.

Hannah Kessel

Cameron Jones

They ask me to write down my race
And I think
and think very seriously
and consider
writing down the truth,
and having my answer read.
I have a man of age.
He is going to school with scars on his back from
the words of people
the same as you and me.
The only difference is Skin
I have his daughter.
all grown up with kids but
there is no husband.
Many years have past,
yet she still lives, but with the LORD.
I have another mother with two children,
this time, she is white.
Her eldest son has traveled to California to try to
take what anyone can and will achieve.
She also lives. Sending her love, every last bit of it,
to her grandchildren.

Hoping with each passing day, to talk to them.

I have a man who works on the field

who has lost one of his most precious possessions

to a thief, who will not feel happiness for the rest of his days

The man physically lives, but life's peace for him has died.

I have a woman who has been wounded

In so many different ways,

I marvel at her strength and will to survive.

She lives with it all. She is the… Wounded Warrior.

I have memories of someone that I can never replace.

I have gone the same path as him.

Though he is my guardian, my role model, my teacher, my friend…

One of the only joys that makes me smile,

Happy if you will,

He is now the Fallen, the taken, the defiled, the murdered.

One of earth's lights that has been put out… but not forgotten.

I have my elder's emotions

I have my father's face

I have my mother's knowledge

I have my brother's teachings in this body.

And I simply

Write down

BLACK

STREETS OF BERKELEY

Madeleine Scott

Bass from the pimp car
Makes my whole body undulate
How I love Berkeley

MATH

Math competitions
Are really a lot of fun
People are haters

BHS CLASSROOMS

I love Berkeley High
Even when the ceiling is
disintegrating

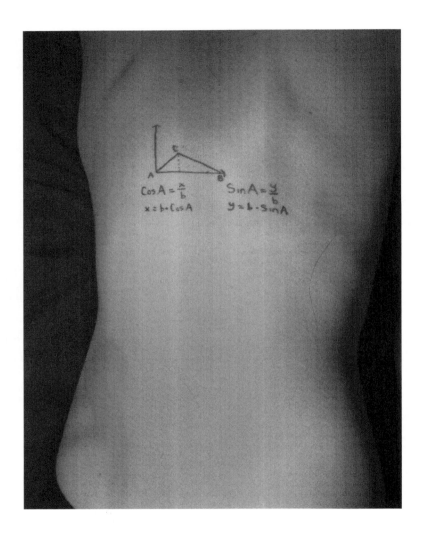

Cara Hunt

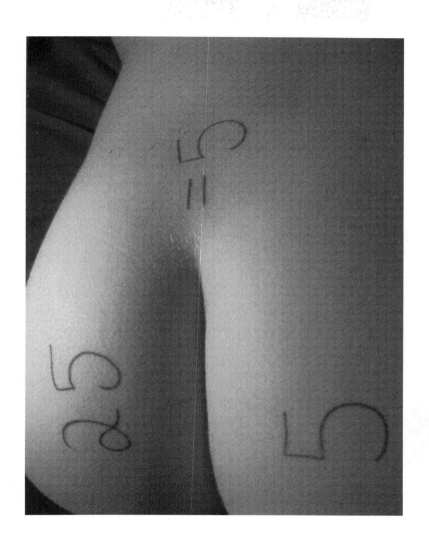

Cara Hunt

FACE EACH OTHER

Richard Raya

I'm out running again. Just through the neighborhood, down towards Prospect Park. It's early, around seven. A Sunday. I love being up at this time of day, only a few other people out, dew drying, birds waking, sun already starting to shine and you can tell, already, that the day will be long and hot and slow.

I suddenly wonder why I'm running. I've been doing it for years now, but I'm starting to wonder if my reasons have changed.

I feel the breeze created by my own speed playing across my exposed skin, my arms, my shins, my chest, my face, wiping away the reforming beads of sweat, cooling. It reminds me of Michelle. She's home right now, sleeping.

I speed up, nearing the park. I plunge in.

Barely anyone awake. Just a few lone birds – doves, I'd like to think – testing the water, indignantly flapping.

OK. There are about three reasons I'm out here, still running.

It's a great feeling to step out of the shower, glance into the mirror, and just be proud of what you see. To be able to answer the door shirtless, to look forward to days at the beach.

It's also a great feeling to… I guess to be someone to look up to. Really, I'm talking about my son. He's also named Richard. The best memories I have of my own dad are of wrestling with him and my brother, fighting, all the way until… well, everyone loses steam at some point. I don't want to, though. I want to stay fresh, stay young, keep everything alive and new, be able to grab my baby boy, who I already know is going to look and act like me, and just toss him high and catch him.

I guess it's embarrassing to admit this last reason to myself – but I want to stay in shape for Michelle. I mean, everyone likes a six pack. But for some reason, Michelle goes crazy for them. When we kiss, we hold each other tight, and her hands just roam, rove across my body, everything taught and smooth. It feels nice. My favorite, though, is when we're just talking, looking at each other, and her fingers slide up and down, across my body, seeping into the grooves between my muscles. I just feel like the luckiest guy, the sexiest man alive, when she does stuff like that to me. It's amazing. Stupid and corny but true.

I nod my head at a young couple – like, younger than us, around college age – they're jogging along at a pretty fast clip in matching track suits. I can't help but snort and shake my head. You can tell just by looking. They're gonna give up soon. They're going too fast, without the right cadence or rhythm, to keep this up for much longer.

It reminds me of when I first started running in high school. "A mile!?" kids would say.

"Yeah," I'd nod, fully aware of the cockiness I was exuding, and reveling in it. "For a warm-up."

"You're insane," people would chuckle in disbelief. All I could do was laugh. Laugh and laugh. I guess I always knew I was one for the long run.

There's a spot up ahead where I like to stop and work out. Bars where I can do pull-ups and soft ground for push-ups and crunches.

I slip out of my tank top, sling it over a bar, and seamlessly, ceaselessly, I slide into my routine. I used to be able to do three sets of ten, back in high school. Today, I do three sets of eleven. Breath in and out, again, the rhythm, the beat that gives me my stamina.

A girl that often comes here walks up. She not-so-subtly shoots me some enticing glances, sets down a mat and starts doing some yoga. I try to stifle a derisive laugh. Yoga people always crack me up.

I admit, I glanced over at her once or twice. She sure seemed to be limber. Her youthful body was svelte, sun-tanned fitness all around. It's not like I'm some decrepit old married dude. I'm only like... what is it now? Twenty-nine? Thirty? Thirty. So yeah. You could say there was some sexual tension. A lone bead of sweat ran from behind her ear down the nape of her neck.

But I'm only half noticing. All that's in my head – maybe because of this random chick – is Michelle. For whatever reason, I can't stop thinking about those nine months Michelle was pregnant. I'd come home from work and she'd be there on the couch, her belly a gourd laden with vast potential. She'd set down the remote as I'd hand her a big box of pizza, a bag of donut holes, and some mangoes. Cravings. I thought they were endearing. I'm a good husband. I'd sit with her and we'd both eat in silence, her head on my shoulder as, depending on who managed to snag the remote, we'd watch chick flicks or superhero cartoons. She loved Spider-Man.

In front of me, the yoga chick reaches her hands behind her and her torso arches in my direction. Convex. Protruding. She lets out a moan of satisfaction. I sit back and take a momentary break from my routine.

When we were first dating, Michelle told me looks were only secondary – that she placed more value on someone's personality. I agreed. I told her I was just the same. But I could tell she felt bashful and embarrassed by her huge size. Like I wouldn't want to touch her anymore. "Don't worry," I'd tell her. "I'm your husband; this is what I'm here for. I'll still wanna fuck you when you're fat."

That was one of the problems with this yoga chick, I decided. Too skinny. Or rather – too afraid to get fat.

It was weird, making love to Michelle when she was pregnant. Me and her, together, with just our future between us. But at the same time, it felt familiar. It took a long time for me to realize what it reminded me of. It reminded me of the first time I had sex which, coincidentally, was with her. The tight embrace, like a hug, my right hand on the small of her back, my left hand behind her head. The long and slow thrusts, gentle really, of back and forth, slow. Staring straight into her face, her eyes, her lips slightly apart, silent words leaking out. The timid carefulness, melting away as we hit our stride and our boundaries began to blur, the mounting ecstasy, the realization that I was able to bring pleasure to the both of us with one unilateral action.

Not even gonna lie. Moments like that... they're some of my favorite things about being married to Michelle. Don't get me wrong – I love the pure emotional stuff, the spending hours holding hands stuff – but it's hard to beat the love making parts. See, the thing is, people who just don't understand try to separate the two. They don't know what it's like. They don't even know what love feels like. Love is like... for me, at least, it feels like being two aspects of the same person. That may be hard to understand. But it's like, this union of interlocking puzzle pieces, this sense that you can't fully know yourself until you get to know this amazing person that's ensnared your mind. It's like two faces of one coin, or the sea and the sky, or the story and

the words. Inextricably bound opposites with ultimately
the same soul. And that's what it feels like, when I'm with
Michelle, sharing those fleeting seconds of passion, writhing
and wiggling together, locked, as for a few glorious seconds
she and I are physically one.

The yoga girl is still stretching, the fabric of her clothes
being pulled tight. I stare straight ahead, concentrating.
Focused.

The sex is just a part of it. Like I said. I love the emotional stuff. And I'm a good husband. She doesn't like
Valentine's Day. Thinks it's stupid, says everyday should
be a day for love. I agree, but I still buy her a bouquet on
Valentine's Day, and some candy. I don't know. I think it's
funny. But I don't stop there. Every day, I tell her I love her.
I know it seems like the obvious thing to do, especially when
you're married – but I just feel like it needs to be said. And
every now and then, I write her something. A letter, a story.
I just sit and try to bottle the rush of feelings that fountain
out whenever I think of her, like an endless geyser spurting
from inside of me. She inspires me. All I do is put words to
it and offer it back, reminding her, again and again, that
what I feel is the truest and most sincere thing I've ever felt.

That's just how I roll, you know? I'm an affectionate
guy. At first, I worried. She's one of those free spirit types,
kind of like me, who loves that spontaneity and loathes the
day things become stagnant. I worried my rhythm would
get too predictable, she would despise my fawning love.
One day, I had to ask her if my constant affection was getting old.

"See, that's the thing about… love," she said, brow furrowed, mouth still open even when she stopped talking, as
if struggling to fit around the simple words, as if she was
surprised at what she was saying. "It never gets old, does

it?"

I had to kiss her, right then. What else can you do, you know?

So, things haven't died down. They're not boring. Things still feel new.

Because honestly, each day is new. Every day is always new and different, whether you're in love, or alone, or anything. No matter who you are, no day is the same as any one before it. In our conceit, we fool ourselves into thinking that things can get routine, that we can learn all we need to know. But... it'll never be like that. Sometimes, you just need the right person to help you understand. To give you the courage to accept the fact that things change, mountains weather and trees fall and lakes dry and beasts of all sizes die. Only that which we assign meaning, that which we imbue with our souls, endures.

I'm done exercising for today. I sling my shirt over my shoulder, give a quick nod to the yoga chick – even though it's not necessary – and set off for home, running swift, energized, passing the young couple from before, now out of breath. I keep running, out of the park and through town, the diners receiving their first real customers and the shops flipping their signs. Little Richard will be asleep when I get home, but Michelle will be awake, in bed, waiting for me. The sun will be climbing and lance in through the window, peaking, jealous, as I lick up the sweat that trickled down her soft beautiful throat to the place that connects the base of her neck to her collar bone, as I run my hands over the gentle luscious swells of her body and just laugh at how amazing I feel. Richard might wake up and toddle in, whispering "ma" or "da-da" or "waffles". And Michelle and I will get up and go to the kitchen, and she'll have to make breakfast because I still don't remember how it's all organized.

Today's Saturday. Tomorrow's Sunday. I'll just do it all, all over again.

The same path, but a different day. That's all I need.

Mai Downs

DEAR VISCOUS AMERICAN CHEESE,

Joseph Brandel

Wikipedia says that your firm stature and full bodied taste: "… does not meet the legal definition of cheese and must be labeled as "cheese product" or similar." And I think that's nonsense. Kraft has been making you with the love of the lord for near a hundred years and you still can't be called cheese! Personally I think America is going to hell. David Letterman got extorted for being Bill Clinton, Obama is Hitler, and the government wants to get their greedy hands all over my Medicare.

Processed cheese is one of the only things I can still believe in. Let me give you an example: My daughter, who I have diligently home schooled for most of her life, (as most Americans should do, schools are full of government propaganda) recently enrolled in Roanoke, Virginia's public school system. I thought I had instilled enough knowledge in her to sort out right from wrong over there, since I have to go take care of my ailing mother (she has diabetes, unfortunately) during the day now, and I cannot teach her any longer. And what happens on the second day of school? She comes home and says at dinner: "Why shouldn't the government take over healthcare? What's wrong with socialism?" I swear I saw the Devil in her gleaming eyes – the little smart ass. They have taken my sweet little girl, who had so recently held the strongest convictions of God's good righteousness and turned her evil! The FBI must have access to Wikipedia. Why is everything I believe in turning upside down? I think I'm a lesbian.

Thank you Cheese,
Cindy Bronwyn

NOCTURNAL

Anna Powelson

THE CONDUCTOR

Bryce Peterson

I should be a conductor, I thought, watching the girl bounce her arms rhythmically up and down and to the side with a confident, fluid sort of motion, like she was swimming through the music. That's great. I've always been very intimate with my music, it would be nice to be able to do that, to be the head of an orchestra like that. I wonder what it would take. Maybe there are some classes you can do or something. I wonder how she got to do it. In a high school band it seems like it would be hard unless you were really good, in which case they'd probably want you on the trumpet or something like that. Maybe she'd just badgered the teacher until she relented. That'd put her up a few notches in my book, no doubt. She gave a few more strokes with her hands and then made a flourish, as if straightening out a piece of string in front of her face, and put her arms by her side. I wish I'd done music when I was in high school.

The band stopped and the game started up again. Danny leaned over to me and pointed at the field.

"Check out number four," he said. "They put him on just now, I think he's gonna try and streak it, he's real fast." The play started but the quarterback was knocked down before the ball ever got to number four. They set back up and did the play over, and this time it got to number four, who dashed through the defense, dodging and jumping, and went thirty yards before being pushed out of bounds.

"I guess high school football is a little different from

professional, huh?" I said. Danny laughed.

It was almost halftime of the long-awaited game between the Helix Highlanders and the Mount Miguel
Matadors, and the Highlanders were leading 14-10. All
the parents and band nerds were in the bleachers and the
minority students were behind the bleachers in a big dirty
area laughing and talking. I think they call that polarization.
One guy in front of me was constantly giving commentary
and cussing to his red-haired wife, who tried not to be af-
fected by it. I'm assuming he was a dad.

I wish I could've played football. Look at them! That's
the essence of American adolescence right there! Those
are a bunch of kids that are spending their time doing
something useful. Everybody here, not just the players. The
band, the students behind the bleachers, they're getting
conditioned, they're growing into themselves. I never went
to football games. I hardly went to high school! If only I'd
known what football games were like, I would've stayed the
full four years.

"Oh man!" said Danny, elbowing me. "What a play!
That number four, jeez..."

"Yeah, that's the secret weapon," I said, but I hadn't
seen. I was busy looking at the conductor. She was just a
high school girl when she wasn't controlling musical traf-
fic. She adjusted her round glasses and took off her gloves,
looking comfortable even though she was standing on a ten
foot pedestal.

"So what do you think they'll try for? Field goal or
touchdown?" he asked.

"Field goal," I said.

"High school football?"

"Ahh," I said. "Ten pro football yards equal thirty high
school football yards. Touchdown." They went for a touch-

down, making it with a smooth pass in the back corner of the end zone. Success. And there were cheerleaders cheering at us, too. They did their little kicks and spins and pom-poms and cheers and then yelled "wooo" and waved and smiled and then turned around. So that's where confidence comes from. I looked behind the bleachers, where a few young couples were making out by the fence. The others formed into little groups.

Halftime came, and I got to see the conductor again. She had a set sort of motions she did with her hand, which was a little disappointing. It would be cool if she just did it freestyle, letting the music flow from some inner well. I bet there are rules for conducting, just like the violin or something. I wonder if City College has conducting classes. Probably not.

Danny went to get a churro at the snack stand. The band had good choreography, doing a sort of war dance with their playing, with shields and swords and flag-bearers doing their own dance. All in all very impressive. I'll bet their college applications look really good, too. Especially the conductor. Being a conductor has to give you some kind of bonus points or something.

"Guess what?" said Danny. "They were out of churros."

"Guess you got there too late."

"They're never out of churros!" he said. "But they were just taking out these pretzels. I got you one."

"Thanks, whoah…"

"Yeah, you can wipe some of that salt off." They'd laid the salt on a little heavy. The game was about to start, and the Matadors were up 17-14. "Oh," he said. "Remember that car we saw going in on the lawn? Yeah, they're selling raffle tickets for it for two bucks."

"Really?"

"Yeah, I guess someone didn't want their old car any-more." The loudspeaker boomed:

"THE RAFFLE FOR THE '93 HONDA ACCORD WILL BE ENDING IN FIVE MINUTES, GO ON AND GET A TICKET NOW, ONLY TWO DOLLARS!"

"You should get one," Danny said. I waved him off.

"What I really need is some water. This is salty, man."

"I don't know where there's a water fountain around here. You could check the bathrooms." I left to search for water, wading through the thick crowd, trying to hold myself as if I belonged, trying to avoid getting bumped into by any of the rambunctious teens. I went past the police officers and security guards, hoping I didn't look suspicious. I always feel like I'm about to get busted for something, I don't quite know why. There was no water to be found, so I went back to the game.

"What happened?" I asked when I got back.

"They got another touchdown," he said.

"Already?"

"Yeah, well we messed up the punt, so they didn't have to take it very far." He shook his head.

"It's alright, we haven't lost to these guys since the 80's." The Matadors intercepted a bad pass and scored another instant touchdown. "Jesus!" said Danny.

"We're done for," I said. "I know the way high school teams work from when I used to play soccer. Once they've passed a certain threshold where they're losing by a certain amount, sportsmanship all goes to hell. They start mak-ing bad plays, it all goes downhill, and the other team gets confident and just starts going off. Look at the young people on our side. They're just talking amongst themselves, see they're distancing themselves from the team, they're saying, 'oh, we're losing, that's just them.'" In pro football we'd be angry right now. We'd be yelling for a comeback. And look at the other side, they're into it, their band's playing in the stands, they're rooting for their team, they're part of it."

"We'll see," said Danny, though he'd stopped listening a while ago. "I'm just trying to watch the game." He furrowed his brow ever so slightly.

Why did I never play football or basketball? I guess I did go to that basketball camp, but that was before I understood the concept of competitive sports. I was just interested in having fun, which translated eventually into not being good at anything. There was that one time at day camp, when I was little, when they were all playing football and I was just watching, and one of them said "how 'bout him, is he good at football," pointing at me. I smiled and someone threw me the ball. All I knew was that you were supposed to get it to the other side so I just ran as fast as I could across the field, jumping away from anyone that tried to get me. "He's hella good!" someone said, and that was the end of my football career.

The Highlanders got worse and worse as the point disparity grew. Danny looked upset and it didn't help that I wasn't upset along with him. I didn't have those same emotional ties to the team that he did. Maybe if I'd stayed at the school I'd have more spirit. I was never really involved in the community, even when I was a part of it.

The third quarter ended, and the loudspeaker announced the winner of the '93 Accord, who accepted the prize with a modest grin.

"I bet you get to keep whatever's in the glove compartment, too!" I joked.

"Yeah, but you also have to pay the taxes and upkeep, and I'm sure the car isn't in perfect shape."

"Yeah," I said, shaking my head.

"WE'D LIKE TO ANNOUNCE SENIOR CHEER-LEADER VICTORIA RAMIREZ. SHE WANTS TO GO TO USC OR LONG BEACH STATE UNIVERSITY, AND SHE'D LIKE TO THANK HER MOTHER, HER BROTHER ROBERT, AND ERIC, WHO HAVE BEEN WITH HER THE WHOLE WAY, LET'S GIVE IT UP FOR VICTORIA!" Victoria led a little cheer and the fourth quarter began. The Matadors started off with another surprise touchdown, facilitated again by number four.

I hope it's based on genes, because that would give me a chance. If it's all about how you grew up, that would be depressing, because it would mean I'd never be able to get emotionally involved in something like this. I'd like to be like everyone else, and I think I was meant to be. I'm usually pretty well-liked, but I just can't quite get into it. If it's in the genes I at least have a chance.

The Highlanders made a field goal and Danny hollered, nudging me victoriously.

There were a lot of awkward kids in the band. I guess that's where they put all the boring ones. I could see all the little social groups forming, the nerd boys getting together with one girl who didn't quite fit in with the rest, a bunch of girls talking, with one boy who didn't quite fit in with the guys, a few singing some old metal ballad, obviously wanting to start a rock band, and arguing over a schnitzel.

The Matadors won 44-17, and their coach was doused with Gatorade. Danny furrowed his brow. It took the band a few seconds to notice that the game was over. With a yell from the conductor, who'd noticed immediately, they started getting their gear together, putting on hats and beginning the march down to the field. While the football players shook hands, they played an end-of-game dirge, and everyone in the bleachers and behind the bleachers slowed down whatever they were doing and started sluggishly towards the exits. Two rows in front of me, an aunt or something talked to a teenage girl, who was smiling and trying her best to answer questions and make jokes and not look strange. She was unforgivably ugly, but she was doing her best.

Phoebe Wong

Shalina Omar

Love and sleep and frustration
swimming swimming drowning sinking
settling at the bottom
looking up from below
mesmerized by swirling columns
of filtered light, sifting sifting
grasping at dust particles that don't exist
and ideas too far out of reach.

pulling daisies and grass like pulling hair
deformed balls of green shoots and roots
smeared onto knees

don't leave me staring at my reflection
whispers whispers, fervent whispers
fogging the mirror
cold kisses reflecting on my lips
like cold metal pressed against my skin

fistfuls of stardust, glittery and iridescent
soft as butterfly wings
crumbling and falling away

a million stars
falling from my skies
like rain into my open hands
and down my neck

let me scream at those stormy heavens
let me feel the fire from my fingertips
because i'm in a vacuum all by myself
the silence and the solitude
breathing in and breathing out

a silence to drive you crazy
a silence to drive you sane

love and sleep and noisy quiet.
my perfect lullaby.

Michaela Bathrick

1

Bryce Peterson

Chapter 1

The boy is sitting down with the girl and they are laughing. The boy is reading aloud from a book, which the girl finds simply hilarious, and they lie down and look at the sky.

Chapter 2

The boy and the girl are eating ice cream at the ice cream store. He got vanilla and she got strawberry. He doesn't like strawberry and she doesn't like vanilla. They are talking and laughing until the ice cream falls off her cone and lands in her lap. She gets very sad but the boy turns it into a joke and she laughs as he cleans her off. She still has a stain but that's okay, and the man who owns the ice cream store likes them for taking it so easy and gives her a free replacement cone. They laugh and eat their ice cream outside.

Chapter 3

The boy is getting on the bus and the girl is standing outside. They've just hugged goodbye and the girl is looking sad but the boy smiles and makes funny faces through the window. Even though the girl smiles and wipes tears away, she still looks sad. He puts his hand on the window and she waves slowly as they part.

2

Chapter 1

The girl is sitting in a pretty meadow. She looks a little bit older, and she is just as pretty, maybe more so. The boy walks up to her and she turns around and smiles. They hug. They sit down across from each other, cross-legged, and mostly he talks and she's silent. He pretends to read a book and laughs but she doesn't smile. He drops an imaginary strawberry ice cream cone in her lap and she doesn't smile. He scratches his chin.

Chapter 2

The boy and the girl are walking through the meadow, and the girl is going more slowly than the boy. The boy looks back to make sure she is still there and talks enthusiastically. He pushes aside some reeds and cattails, and they see a beach. They sit down and the boy points everywhere. He touches her on the shoulder and points to the sky, putting his arms out to show the vastness of everything. She looks up and the sun makes her eyes look shiny, even after she shades them with her hand. She looks at him and tosses a handful of sand in the air, which is blown away by the wind and scatters. He looks at her with a smile and tosses a handful of sand into his mouth, swallows most of it, and laughs.

Laurel Wee

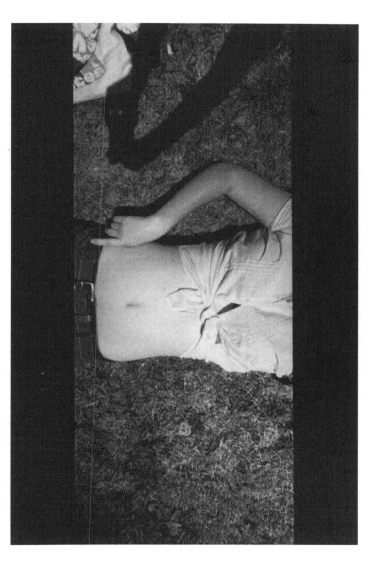

Noelani Blumenfeld-Honea

EPIC-LESS

Zach Wilson

"I've never understood the phrase 'grasp something so tightly your knuckles turn white.' Mine get white when I make a loose fist."

This marked the end of the last interesting story William Harper ever told me. Willie was a tall, skinny man who I went to college with. He was fairly good looking with a surprisingly strong jaw for a guy his slight of frame.

Willie had just finished telling me the story of the incident that allowed him to sue the company he used to work for. Apparently, Willie made a joke under his breath about the infidelity of his boss's wife (or rather how Willie had slept with her the night before, he hadn't, but Willie was annoyed with his boss.) Little did he know his boss's spouse had just left him. Loathing life and sick of being pushed around, his boss snapped and started to strangle Willie. Which brought him to the phrase, 'grasp something so tightly your knuckles turn white.' The something in this situation just happened to be Willie's neck. His coworkers quickly jumped in and pried the boss's hands from Willie's collar.

Despite bruises on his neck and the need to drink all food in liquid form for the next three weeks, Willie was very content to have been strangled. Maybe it was because he was quitting a job he thoroughly despised or that he "earned" (as he put it) 5.6 million dollars (after the lawyer fees) from this affair. Either way, he told me he felt like Edward Norton in Fight Club while leaving the office. Smugly humming (he wouldn't be able to whistle again for two weeks) to himself, he carted away his things, indifferent to the large red marks on his neck.

An extremely conservative man, financially speaking, Willie put most of his money in a bank. Many people would go on vacation or buy something special if they happened upon a large sum of cash, but not Willie. He said, "I want to live off this money for the rest of my life." With the way he spends his money, he could do it.

I have no idea what he does with his free time. Maybe he tries to write a book or a series of short stories about all of the zany bosses he had at his various jobs. He always has considered himself a literary person.

What made Willie interesting to talk to, or rather to listen to, was that he always had great stories. Over his 39 years of existence, he has worked at a multitude of jobs. Everything from an audio technician to a zookeeper. The common denominator of all of these jobs was his boss. His boss was, always, I mean every goddamned time, either mean, dumb, or incompetent. On rare occasions he was all three combined. When I would see him, he would have outrageous stories about how dim-witted his boss was or how he had undermined his boss's authority. One of his bosses stood on a table to show the success of his new diet. Broke the table. Broke his leg. Another time, after receiving an unjustifiably poor performance review, he made 500 business cards identical to his boss's in every way except for one. He made the email ihaveatinydick@mac.com. He secretly switched these new business cards with his boss's old ones. His boss, a devout catholic and Steve Jobs hater, greatly disliked these new cards when he eventually realized

they had been changed. It was puerile, I know, but hilarious
nonetheless. Willie was never caught, but he was fired for
stealing pens and post-its three weeks later.

Willie's deep, rich voice would captivate my mind. Full
of passion and intensity, his words would spin a tale for me
in my head. Whenever I would see him there would be a
fable, a legend, an epic. We rarely talked of his life beyond
work, let alone anything involving me. But it was fine for
both of us. I gained a story and he gained someone who
would actually listen to him. It was a routine. He would
come to my apartment about once a week and weave a nar-
rative. His boss's assault changed that.

Success doesn't suit Willie, never has, probably never
will. Despite being destined for wealth, he would be better
off in the working class. Going to his job everyday, something to complain about. But fate had a different plan for
him. Without a boss he has nothing to lament, no stories to
tell, nothing to say except for boring commentaries on the
decline of modern cinema. "Where are the Bogarts?" he
said during the only time I saw him since his strangling.

"Where are the Kellys? The Newmans! The Pecks! The
Gables! Who is there now? Nicholson and Hackman are
old. There is no one."

"What about Day-Lewis or Hoffman?" I retorted.

"Where are the Brandos?" he replied.

I haven't seen him since. It's been over five years. I
called him once. Told him he should take a vacation. Who
knows if he listened? Sometimes I wonder what he does,
what he's thinking. Whether he did take that vacation or got
another job. He probably didn't do either. Does he wallow
in his own sadness, his own loneliness? Has he realized that
he needs structure in his life? Maybe. He stews in a pool
of his self-pity. That's likely what he's doing. That's how I

imagine him, sitting at a typewriter, reruns of Sportscenter on the T.V., coming to the conclusion that his life lacks fulfillment and is completely meaningless. Maybe I should call him again…

Sasha Jacobs

BEAUTY

Arielle Scharff

A parasite. That's what she was. But as soon as she injected her words into me, there was no getting rid of her. I like to think it happened some stormy day in December. I like to think that I was minding my own business, innocently carrying on with my work when she sunk her vicious teeth into my neck, pricked me with her spindle, fed me her poison apple. I like to think I put up a fight, tooth-and-nail, to prevent her wrathful eyes from boring into me.

But I know the truth. I know I was waiting for something – anything – that could change me, change my life. I welcomed her slithering tentacles over my arms; I was immediately captivated by her enchanting promises.

Seventh grade. While everyone else was worried about whether they would fit in, I was worried about how to stand out. I was already getting an A in the smart math class, seeing local bands on weekends, wearing dark clothes, and planning my bat mitzvah. But anyone could do that. It didn't take any effort on my part, and I still went mostly unnoticed by the cute boys and popular girls.

That's when she reminded me of the ultimate achievement, the highest attainable quality, the one thing that would set me apart from the masses of public school. Beauty.

She showed me the way, enlightened me, guided me through each day. My first lesson was on calories. First, though, I had to be initiated into her lifestyle. I stood in front of the mirror and pledged allegiance to hating everything about my reflection.

And so it began. Every morning, she lovingly guided my hand away from the milk to the water, from the cereal to the crackers, where I'd eat my daily ration of three. During the day, when my stomach complained, her biting words put it to rest: "Eat your fat. You have enough to live off of. You're lucky I let you eat anything."

At lunch, she let me eat my apple, drink my water, munch on my celery, and sometimes even savor a slice of bread. At dinner, she let me eat most of what was on my plate.

Seventh grade passed, summer passed, and eighth grade began. By then, her cancerous cells had spread through my brain, until her thoughts and mine were inseparable. My feeble body shuddered in protest each time she and I dragged it out of bed to go for a run. My mouth ignored my protests and ate and ate. This made her angry, and I soon found myself kneeling over the toilet, tickling the back of my throat.

Nowadays, she isn't as much of me. I expelled her from my mind, as much as I could. Sometimes, I hear a faint echo of her raging shout. I tune her out. I eat what I want.

Olivia Page

ONE

Tahryn Smith

Some days just feel like this.

The heat wraps around you

Thick, a heavy blanket on your

Bare shoulder.

Holding you, holding it in.

An attempt,

And almost-gasp

Silent, lungs pulling in the

Vaporous air of summer

Like cement blocks in your chest.

Despondent.

Thin black lines on paper

That you tear, crumple, toss

As you search the nothingness

For a something, a meaning, a truth.

And you talk to yourself

The sound of your tongue in your mouth

Like the enormous slap of a wave

Reverberates off the walls and

You begin to cry for something

Lost, but what?

Nothing was ever truly yours

To begin with.

TWO

Deep green feeling

Sticky and sweet

Pinky toes, eskimo kisses

and the first week of Spring

when the cage inside you opened

And filled the glistening air

with all the things

that made the crowd gasp with delight.

Windblown, sun-warmed skin

blossom cheeks.

ripping off layer after layer

after layer

in a race towards

Lightness.

a desperate attempt.

As white teeth

bite pink tongues

and pink lips

biding time.

a volatile, youthful

kind of waiting.

Our numbered days of freedom

each sticky and sweet seemingly

endless.

Evan Neff

Eugenio Geiken

I've been sent on a mission, to tell you that none of this matters. That the world we live in is merely a speck of existence within a space that is unimaginably large. I feel obligated to tell you about the mysteries that lie beyond our sky.

It began with a dream, a pleasant dream; a dream that made mind depart from skull, skull from body, and then, eventually, body from earth. I was carried gently above the planet with eyes closed. As I raised my eyelids, slowly but surely, a mystical light seeped into my field of vision. By the time my eyes were open wide, I could see into the deepest corners of this visible, starlit space. These stars were shimmering brightly, beckoning me for a visit into their vibrant domain. At that moment, my journey began.

It seemed as though I wasn't moving through space, but that space was moving toward me. I was suspended, fully erect, with galaxies and nebulas as my guide. But I know I'm not the only one who has experienced this. You have too.

Can you recall the first time your mind was blasted by the spiral galaxy, with its pink and blue light filtering through the black, velvet space in a whirlpool of stars and planets? Can you recall that spectacle? Or have your thoughts been wiped clean by what's been going on in your heart and mind? Let me reassure you that these amazing destinations haven't faded away. We've both experienced this together, and we will continue to for another aeon.

So why can't you remember? I was almost certain the feelings were mutual. When 10,000 years ago, a star in the constellation Cassiopeia began to supernova, and space bled fluorescent green and red; sulfur and oxygen scattered all around us. Wasn't that memorable? Didn't you feel the pulsing energy channel through your body as your eyes beheld such a sight? A feeling as smooth and comforting as your skin that left me breathless as I bathed in the Eagle nebula.

But without you, space is overwhelmingly empty, and I'd rather die than feel this lonely.

Mai Downs

Mai Downs

Joseph Brandel

I am excited and challenged by the work in this class. Ms. Branderbishop, the new english teacher, a real doll, is the sort that gives you a nice grade just for being yourself. And even though I could easily schmooze my way through the class, she actually gives some pretty interesting work – the sort of stuff that is relevant to even the most jaded, disinterested teenagers like myself.

Now don't get me wrong, I'm an intelligent guy, but at this point I'm beyond doing work. In my defense, it is senior year and very few people actually do their work. Her first assignment was simply to make a list with a variety of things, unconventional or not, that we wanted to do before we graduated and probably moved away from home. Normally this would just be a boring exercise for classmates to meet each other at the beginning of each year, but with the inclusion of the word "unconventional," something required by the school actually became a little fun. Here's the list I wrote:

TO DO LIST: SEPTEMBER 13, 2007

- Take out the trash
- Buy 14 tabs of ecstasy
- Take bath (not shower)
- Go to store, buy icy hot pads
- Eat cheesiest quesadilla EVER
- Redefine rock 'n roll

- Stack bills
- Inherit real estate
- Deposit Xmas check
- Investigate caves
- Finish 2 year old photo project, so I can go to college
- Eat a super burrito once a week
- Pass Pre-calc
- Acquire stream of consciousness
- Read some Trotsky...AND
- Avoid young Stalin.

Dennis Wornick

Dennis Wornick

Jonathan Ruchlis

Over the course of human history, there have been many questions that are constantly debated but never answered with complete certainty. "Evolution or Creation?" and "Fate or Free Will?" are just a couple of examples. Although these questions may never have concrete answers, it is human nature to try and tackle them anyway. I often feel the urge to try to answer these questions, and there is one question that stands out as more complicated and puzzling than all the rest. If pitted against each other, who would win: Batman or James Bond? And I'm not talking about putting them in the ring together for a fistfight. If both of them got to use the extent of their resources and skills, which one of them would successfully demonstrate superiority over his opponent? The urge to tackle this question has become too strong to overcome. I have to think it through and make my decision.

Batman and Bond actually share a lot of qualities. They are both age-old beloved characters with countless movies and books about them. Although he is considered a superhero, Batman doesn't actually have any super-human powers, and, of course, neither does James Bond. They both rely on their fighting expertise, their talents as detectives, and the technologies that are designed for them, either by Lucius Fox or the British Government. They both go head to head with dangerous criminals using their own unique tactics, and they both like to do things their way. Neither is great at taking orders.

When tackling a question like this one, I have to assess the advantages and disadvantages on both sides. I'll start with their cars. Bond seems to have a new car for each mission, generally an Aston Martin tricked out with all sorts of guns, tracking devices, bulletproof windows, etc. Batman, on the other hand, has always driven around in the Batmobile. The Batmobile changes a bit from movie to movie but consistently has an extremely strong, bulletproof exterior, a high tech computer, and its fair share of guns. Although Bond definitely has the advantage of keeping a low profile, something that can't be done in the Batmobile, and his cars are equipped with many more features, in a head to head crash the Batmobile would come out on top. Bond has the backing of the British Government on his side, but Batman has his secret identity, which could be a problem for Bond when trying to seek Batman out and kill him. It's safe to say that Bond has the better gadgets, but Batman has his bat suit, which makes him less vulnerable to gunfire or other weapons, and gives him the ability to fly, or at least fall very slowly. They are both incredibly smart, and would surely devise extremely clever plans to debilitate each other.

It would be a long battle, involving many failed attempts on both ends. James Bond would probably discover Batman's secret identity fairly quickly and try to catch him off guard, but he would be surprised by Batman's agility, and would soon be facing him in full armor. There would probably be a number of fights, none of them very definitive, and perhaps a car chase or two. But I think it would most likely end with an unexpected attack from the sky, with Batman swooping in from the top of a building and knocking Bond unconscious. Since Batman isn't much of a killer, I'd guess that he would take Bond prisoner. And although Bond might escape from captivity, as he has many times before, I doubt he would be able to come back and defeat Batman in a second round of play. Batman would be crowned the winner of their battle.

Shannon Miller

PULCHRITUDINOUS

Jamie Lin

The first thought that popped into his mind was that she was pulchritudinous.

He'd been scared, the days before he was set to meet her, for reasons unknown to him. After all, logic determined that she was bound to be more than beautiful. And even if she wasn't, he would love her all the same. Without even meeting her, he knew he would love her wholly and unconditionally, because even if she was ugly, he knew she was a gorgeous person on the inside. She had to be, because from the little he knew of her there was no other way for her to be.

He'd told his best friend of his fears, and she had assured him, with that little eyeroll of hers at his ridiculousness, that his fears were unnecessary and of course she would be beautiful, you idiot. But then she'd launched into one of her typical tirades about how beauty was in the eye of the beholder and not the most important aspect of a person, lectures he'd heard from her a million times and could probably quote from memory. He begrudged her in slightly resentful silence, since his best friend was pregnant, after all, and that did give her some excuse for being moody and grumpy all the time.

He was only able to bear his best friend's grumpiness of late with the thought that it would all be over soon. Soon, his best friend would no longer be pregnant, and he'd no longer have to listen to her complaints or whines or ridiculous cravings or any of the things that she had bugged him with the past nine months. He'd be free of her tirades about beauty and the follies of man and all the other topics she needed to rant about every day. He'd be free of her own fears and doubts and needs for reassurance that yes, she was still beautiful, and yes, he wouldn't make fun of her for being fat.

All that was over now, thankfully, and more importantly, it was all worth it, as he held their daughter and the first thought that popped into his mind was that she was pulchritudinous.

Shelby Abeles

Annelise Finney

GROWTH, PLANTS, AND US

Vivian Ponte-Fritz

Flicking fingernails too long too short, it hurts as I hit them against the rails.

Child sucking on the corner of a silken blanket. Becoming pot bellied big human standing cornered in the open street to beat

To respond to the beats

Coming around the chipped and graffiti stained bend, spilling out of the cracks in the cement, out of the bent car painted brightly.

Too much for the rest of this grey and getting greyer neighborhood. Almost as hollow and blank as my angry grandfather's left, blind eye. The one that stares, discontentedly, at young lovers in the park.

Spitting an insult through his dentures

Forgetting his own youthful ventures or maybe they were

misadventures.

His drying, crying, loud old mouth never speaks or spits a
sound about a forgotten past. I know that every day I live,
enjoying myself or yelling into grass or dirty pillowcases,
I'm just adding a flower to the vase that will become the
bouquet that I will someday throw behind me

and that, sadly, I will never remember each petal that made
me smile.

Sasha Jacobs

YOU KNOW THAT I LOVED AND HATE AND WILL REALIZE

Jamie Lin

You know that once
upon a time,
butterflies landed in my hair
even if I never saw or felt them
I knew they did,
that their silky rainbow wings slowed as they alighted
and my hair sparkled from the sudden burst of color.
I know they loved me because
I loved them
and together we were pretty friends
and I would never harm them.

You know that now
upon the threshold of adulthood,
butterflies and all other creatures run away from me
and my untamed hair and clawing hands,
even though I see and hear them run,

their eyes fear-crazed and legs skedaddling
and my smile twisted into a sadistic smirk.
I know they run because
I lash out at them
and together we hate endlessly
and I can always harm them.

You know that someday
upon the age of post-disillusionment,
butterflies will not land in my hair
even if I spot them and lie still awaiting,
I know they will not,
that their fragile color-splashed wings are too heavy a bur-
den
and my hair dulled and roughened from knowledge.
I know they will fly away because
I cannot
and together we will realize this is how life is
and I will do harm but not always on purpose.

Abby Wurtele

WORK

Sayre Quevedo

You

Mister or Miss

signed dollar bill diploma

Mister or Miss

College fund cashed,

reading Kerouak

Mister or Missus

Proletariat

but never picked up anything

heavier than a pen

Your America is built

on the backs of my ancestors

So, bend

Bend until your spine splinters,

Bones buckle

Pack bricks, grind granite.

Bend.

Bend.

Bend.

Anonymous ancestors watch:

grid-iron girders balanced

across the blades of your back.

Bend

until your muscles burning

singe the hair on your hands

Bend

beneath the sun

Sow.

Sweat.

Swing

that sledgehammer.

Bend low

beat

the dust from the dirt,

salt from the seafloor

Bend

And while you're at it

bend some more

Abby Wurtele

Shalina Omar

she stared down her reflection in the full length mirror
daring it to say something
to justify its presence
to stop the shivering.
she stared it down and remembered the heat
of scalding water
drumming tell-tale tattoos into her skin.
she remembered her naked body
raw from soap and scrubbing
pink from her attempts at purification
at decontamination.
she remembered the salt that stung her eyes
which glared past the foggy glass.
she remembered the pleas on her lips
which begged to be clean.
she remembered this and dared her eyes to
look away.

Abby Wurtele

I HEART HOT RICE BALLS FROM OAKLAND

Joseph Brandel

Nothing is safe in Oakland. But if you don't know what a hot rice ball is, then get the fuck out! It's inebriating; it'll leave you gaping open. In Oakland, every time the sun sets on the ghetto and all the broken stuff gets cold, murder is the slogan – but if you don't know what a hot rice ball is, then get the fuck out! Every year like clockwork on September 25th, Oakland's Korea-town holds the Harvest Moon Festival on a strip of Telegraph Avenue. The proprietors of neighborhood restaurants serve the most delicious hot rice balls in a sort of red bean porridge called p'at-chuk and the kooky Korean broads put on bunny hats and do dances in the street. It's some surreal shit.

I live about 8 blocks away on San Pablo and Athens and I'll be honest, my house is a real dump. Big warehouse, 12 tenants, and I guess you could say it's spacious... But surely your living room doesn't smell like piss and marijuana all the time. Yeah, they're not exactly ideal roommates. And I'll be honest with myself, the food selection around here is not choice. There's a burger joint across the street called Big Papa's. They boast a gigantic menu, but there's only one thing on the menu that's actually in stock, burger and fries, and it probably comes out of one big bag. They don't even have soda, so rest assured Big Papa's is ghetto as hell.

I stopped going there when I saw the owner man himself, Big Papa, shopping for his produce at the liquor store. That shit is like five days old. There's a Philly cheese steak place about three blocks down San Pablo on 26th. I usually get the jalapeños, mayo, lots of cheese, and half a cow sandwich, but it sits in your stomach like a brick. That place is pretty decent, cheap too. But if I'm gonna level with my audience in a completely honest way, I would have to say that the hot rice balls are not only the best food in my neighborhood, but perhaps even the best food in the city. Maybe because they're only good once a year at the Harvest Moon Festival — because those goddamn restaurants go back to serving BBQ the next day, but I swear to god, once a year I'm reminded by those hot rice balls that it's nice to live here.

Anonymous

I like
Sex

balloons,

f
l
o
a
t
i
n
g

there are post-it notes?

Isaac Pollan

At first, the paper burns blue and green, until it folds in upon itself, turning to ash. The logs begin to catch and illuminate the dark room in an orange glow. The living room closes in around the radiating heat, until the room feels no bigger than the scope of the flickering fire. Clutching blankets to our bodies, my mother and I sit together one cozy night, my father off to New York on business. While the snow embraces the house, we play.

As we listened to the fire begin to smolder and die, my mother got up, saying she would be right back; I should put another log on. She left her cards face down on the floor. I picked up a log and placed it on the hot coals and returned to where I had sat. As I fidgeted with my hands, I became fixated on the glossy back of my mother's cards, shimmering in the firelight. I wondered what secrets she had in her hand and, with a ping of shame, I realized I could find out easily.

With one reluctant flick, I revealed my mother's cards. There were no pocket aces or flushes, just a few fives, a queen, and a seven. I had put myself in moral jeopardy for... chump cards. I heard my mother's footsteps, returned her cards and sat back down.

My mother looked at me. I looked at her, and crawled into her arms. The once small pit in my stomach grew until it engulfed me. I hugged her tight, so tight she began to squirm, and I clawed my hands into her back. I raged at my own tarnished character. The tears came. It was too late. I had tipped my hand; I had to tell.

APOLOGIA

Julian Jaffe

I've been called a lot of things, but I'm here to set the record straight. Although most of the besmirchment of my good name is utterly false and incorrect, I must admit that at least one of these affronts bares a shred of truth: I am, indeed, a know-it-all.

While many find this quality off-putting, to say the least, I believe that it is not a term of opprobrium but of fact, for while I have never claimed to know it all, I do know most of it, and enough to make up the rest. There are some who find my out-of-hand dismissals irritating, but really, if you're wrong, you're wrong. No sense beating around the bush. It's really not my fault if you proceed to utter falsehoods. You can't blame me for wanting to set the record straight. In reality, I am doing you a favor by disabusing you of your notion. Unfortunately, not everyone sees it my way.

I guess I'm not completely blameless. I do lord my knowledge over people, but never intentionally (okay, only rarely). And I understand why some people may be confused and angered by my seemingly bottomless well of trivial and not-so-trivial knowledge. It's only natural for people to distrust what they can't understand.

Finally, I apologize for the real reason that my know-it-allness is a problem: it just makes me so damn smug. So, please accept my heartfelt regrets that I am indeed a know-it-all. But also, please accept that there is a cause, and a simple cure. Just don't be wrong.

LOVE

Jenna Archer

Faggot. Dyke. Homo. We deal with it. At some point, it doesn't even matter; you've already stripped us down to the bone.

Sometimes, people are left with nothing but their pride. Sometimes, people are left with nothing. That's when people kill themselves, that's when they get married.

I have more pride than that, though, which is why I'm here now telling you I love you.

I love you.

You can tell me I'm sick, you can tell me that I'm a fucking fag who's going straight to hell. Shut up. You don't know anything. I've already been in hell. The moment I saw you, something opened up inside my chest, inside my lungs, inside my heart. A great chasm that couldn't be filled with anything except you. I never knew that emptiness could fill a person, I always thought that it was the absence of feeling. But this emptiness, this longing for you, has filled my bones, and even when I pass you in the hallway, I can feel it tingling. This emptiness has consumed me, like a black hole, sucking me into hell, where I will always burn for you. It has filled my stomach. It jolts whenever I see you; it makes me almost sick with joy to be near you.

You can laugh, you can curse, you can say nothing at all. I've seen it all, heard it all before. Just please, don't say you'll pray for me. I can handle your hatred, but I don't want your pity, because I would never change how I feel about you, because that feeling has become a part of me.

Will Parsons

how long since
I kissed your hair
tangled
together in the frantic
silent
passion of possibilities
running
out?
affection
has not taken with it
the taste
or
scent of you
from
me
salt and perfume
a stopper full of chemists'
calculations
holding you
utterly inaccessible
an insoluble
omnipresent
odor
on the edge
of my
memory

Emma Carlblom

Thoughts are crashing into empty space
that surrounds our heads
artifical light beaks into the mirrors of our minds
Our thoughts are becoming mundane
But we don't notice as our emotions fade
And our brainwaves sink into the bottom of the ocean

WHOLE MILK

Sophia Matano

"Harold. Harold, for goodness sakes, Harold. What am I supposed to do with this?" Linda slammed the plastic bottle of milk on the kitchen table.

"There's hardly a difference, Linda," Harold sighed.

"He says there's no difference. Of course there's a difference! Difference in taste, in texture, in —"

"Everyone drinks skim milk. It was a mistake, alright?"

"No, Harold, it's not alright. I'm supposed to put this watered down shit in my coffee? Hell no. You've got another thing comin' if you think I'm puttin' this shit in my coffee."

"I'll get you another, Linda."

"You're gettin' whole milk, *that's* what you're gettin'." She held out a shaking hand, clutching the bottle. Harold took it and kissed his wife on the forehead.

"I'll be back soon," he said softly. Her stern expression cracked and the wrinkles around her mouth drew up around her smile like delicate lace curtains.

Harold shuffled toward the door, stopping to check for his keys and wallet (including the receipt for the milk) before making his way down the three steps leading up to his white house, lined with a chipping blue paint, applied unevenly.

The supermarket was a comfortable six blocks away; short enough for a walk but far enough to be out of the house for an hour or more.

He walked at a brisk pace for his age. He knew every

cross street, every house, every crack in the sidewalk and ticked everything off:

Dellasanta's house, Norko's house, Tuckerman's, Riso's, Whitney St., one way, cross. Theiling's, Lambino's, hand print in the sidewalk, Crosby (say hello to Charles outside), Bailie's, cross Pace St., and up one past the construction, then back. Apartments with that nice Bulgarian family on the second floor, new pavement, Raul's Liquor store, the community center, Mattier house, back to old pavement, cross busy intersection (look both ways twice) at Laurel St…

When the houses and the people coming in and out of them got less familiar, Harold stopped ticking them off. *Not because my memory is failing*, he said to himself, *it's only because I've never met these people.* He returned a smile to a stranger who waved to him.

"Hello Harold!"

"Good morning!"

Not because I'm losing my memory…I'm just very popular.

Once at Desmond's Grocery, he marched down the aisle to the refrigerated dairy section. Approaching the milk section, he readjusted his glasses on his sloped nose. He squinted, his nose an inch from the bottles.

"Do you need help finding something, sir?"

A young man smiled down to him.

"No, no, I'm quite capable of getting some whole milk, thank you very much," Harold peered at him disapprovingly. *Youth today,* he tutted. *Always think they're so superior.*

"Sir, you're holding skim milk."

"You think I don't know that?"

"I'm sorry."

"I'm returning it. For whole milk." Harold could just make out a little smile on the young man's face. "Say, listen, you," Harold pointed a wrinkled finger at the man. "Just because I'm old don't mean I don't know which way's up. I made a mistake, but my vision's better than yours. What you see at 10 feet, I see at 100. I was in the Air Force. You ever been in the Air Force, son?"

"I can't say that I have," he admitted.

"Clearly not," Harold said, eyeing the bright blue smock and name tag pinned to his chest that said *Mark*.

"I'm only working here part-time."

"And what do you do with the rest of your time, Mark? Spark doobies?" Mark chuckled, his cheeks turning rosey. "That's what I thought."

"I'm an artist."

Harold looked up to him above his frames. "What's the difference?"

Mark laughed. Harold started to laugh but only managed a wheeze. He coughed, trying to pass the lump in his throat.

"I'm Mark." He extended a hand.

"Harold Pokallas." Harold shifted the container of milk to his left hand so he could properly shake.

"Well, Mr. Pokallas," Mark grabbed a container of whole milk from the shelves, "let's ring you up."

Harold followed him to the cash register and handed over the old receipt.

"And that should do it!" Mark put the whole milk in a paper bag and passed it over the register.

"Thank you."

"Mr. Pokallas… artists don't just spark doobies."

"They also work at grocery stores."

Mark laughed. "Yeah, in some cases. But I teach a class at the community center, and we have some stuff on display."

"Do you, now?"

"If you ever have some spare time, you should stop by."

Passing the Mattier house, he saw the door to the community center propped open. Two boys dribbling basketballs sprinted past Harold and into the center, startling him.

"Christ!" He clutched his milk close to him to avoid dropping it.

He stood in front of the community center, staring at the red brick façade and grey awning.

"Sir?"

"Huh?"

A woman came out of the center and approached him.

"Can I help you, sir?"

"No, you cannot." Harold squinted at her through his glasses, trying to look menacing.

"You looked lost, I just thought I might —"

"I don't need any of your help, lady. I know exactly where I am. That building, that one over there? That's Raul's Liquor, and that's the apartment where the nice Bulgarian family is. Then that's Pace St., and on the corner is where Lewis Bailie and his family…"

"My mistake." She turned to leave, but Harold cleared his throat.

"Ma'am?"

She looked over her shoulder. "Yes?"

"Is there a Mark…a Mark who works in there?"

"Oh, Mark! Yes, he teaches figure drawing and basketball. He's very popular around here."

"Is there any of his art up? I would very much like to see it."

"There's Mark's personal work and some of his students' drawings."

"Thank you." Harold looked down at his blue lace-up

sneakers.

"I could show you, sir."

"I can find it myself."

"Room 26."

"Thank you."

His grocery bag swinging beside him, he walked down the linoleum hallway. Room 23, 24, 25, 26...

He opened the door to find an office. Next to the door was a large bulletin board with flyers and advertisements. Framed on the wall were paintings, watercolors, sketches, and even the occasional finger-painting. Harold wasn't even sure what color the walls were. They were completely dusted with paper of different sizes.

Making his way around the room, he found figure sketches on the bulletin board. He was a little startled to see that they were all of naked men and women. He moved to the left quickly, averting his gaze.

It took him two minutes to realize that he was looking at the bulletin board, which was not, as he had originally believed, a large collage. He squinted his eyes, trying to make out the writing on one flyer. It read: "Are you a beautiful person? Have your friends commented on how perfect your face and body are? Are you really good at keeping still? Become a NUDE MODEL for the figure drawing classes!"

Harold gasped. How strange.

"It doesn't matter how young or old you are (we lied, you must be over 18) – we want to draw YOU! Earn $45 per session. Call MARK..."

Harold backed away from the bulletin board. He glanced at his watch, realizing how much time he had spent. *Linda will be waiting.*

He looked to his right at the figure drawings. One man

was sitting in a chair.

They paid this man $45 to sit in a chair? What a terrible pose. His posture is abysmal. No excuse. Youth, today. Yeesh.

And with one swift movement, he tore a phone number off the bottom of the flyer and pocketed it.

"Harold! Harold, I swear to God, what could've possibly taken you so long?"

"I stopped by the community center."

"We got a community centa?" Linda grabbed the grocery bag out of his hands.

"Next to the Mattier's house."

"The who?"

"The Mattier family."

"Jesus Christ, Harold! This milk is warm. It's probably goddamn *cream* by now. Or *yogurt*. If I wanted yogurt I woulda asked for it, Harold."

"Stick it in the fridge, it'll be fine."

"What the shit were you doin' at the community centa?"

"I was looking at some art."

"At the community centa? What took you so long?"

"I was looking around!"

"It's not the fuckin' MoMA, Harold. They ain't got fuckin' Picasso in there or nothin'."

"Some kid named Mark told me to look around. He teaches some classes there."

"A kid? Harold, why would you go?"

"I don't know, Linda, Jesus!"

Linda whirled around and grabbed Harold by the shoulders. "Harold. Harry. You're losin' it."

"I'm perfectly fine, Linda."

"You're senile."

"I'm saner than you!"

"C'mere Harry. Follow me." Linda led him to the bath-room and turned the taps of the bathtub. "You need a bath. You need a nice, calming bath. He goes with a strange man to the community centa…"

"I didn't go with him, I went on my way home!"

"You're delusional! Shh!" She fiddled with the knobs of the bathtub, adjusting the temperature. "Now, honey, if you need anythin', I'll be right in the kitchen…Walkin' around in the sun all day, of course you're goin' nuts. All my fault, really, I'm a terrible wife, makin' you walk all the way to Desmond's TWICE…"

Harold sat in the bath, watching his wrinkly body get wrinklier. He sat up as straight as he could, arching his back.

This is how you sit up straight…kids today have gotten lazy. They wouldn't take this in the Force… I could show those kids how models should sit.

He pulled the plug and let the water drain slowly from around him. It sloshed back and forth as a whirlpool around the drain formed, spinning and spinning until the drain gurgled. He summoned some strength and hoisted himself out of the bathtub, his knees knocking together. He stepped out carefully on the pink fluffy mat, his towel wait-ing for him on the sink.

Hell, I could model. I could model the hell out of 'em. They wouldn't know what hit 'em, and they'd see a real pose.

He grabbed the towel and began to dry himself off. Once he was dry, he wrapped the towel around himself, then opened the door.

He peeked out of the bathroom into the hallway. He couldn't see Linda in the kitchen or the bedroom. He stepped out into the hallway and let the towel fall.

Turning his head to the left, he struck a pose, leaning against the wall with one arm.

Now there's a pose!

"Harold, how was your – OH CHRIST ALMIGHTY." Harold looked up to find Linda in the bedroom, covering her eyes.

"Linda!"

"Harold, what are you doin'?!"

"Walking down my hallway naked, Linda, what's it look like?"

"You've lost it, Harold. Completely lost it. Oh Lord…"

"Linda, Jesus, no one can see!"

"So I'm no one, eh?" She dropped her hands from her eyes and held one out to obscure her view of Harold's privates.

"I meant the neighbors, what do you care?"

"It's not right, Harold! You're not supposed to look at people naked."

"Why ever not, Linda? Huh?"

"If I have to explain it to you, Harold, you're beyond help!"

"Linda –"

"Put some fuckin' pants on, Harold!" she screamed, throwing his khaki pants to him.

They landed at his feet. He stared at them, crumpled on the floor. He looked up to Linda who jabbed a wrinkled finger at the pants, glaring.

He picked up the pants, defeated. He stepped into them uneasily, and then put his legs in slowly, careful not to fall, one after the other. He zipped up his fly, then held up his hands.

"Good. Now, what do you want for dinna? I was thinkin' we could do some pasta with marinara sauce. I wanted to do pesto, but we're out of pine nuts…" She shimmied her way past him into the kitchen. He followed her silently, putting his hands in his pockets.

"Of course, we could always do a cream sauce, you like cream sauce? Harold?"

"Huh?"

"Cream sauce or marinara?"

Harold stood still in the doorway. In his right pocket, he felt something itching his index finger. He pulled out a tiny slip of paper.

"Harold? Harry?"

He unfolded it, revealing Mark's phone number. He smiled. His wrinkles spread across his entire face.

"Up to you, darling." He cupped her head in his hands and kissed her on the forehead.

He picked up the phone receiver on the wall and began to dial.

"Harold? Who are calling? Harold?"

"Hello, is this Mark? Hi, Mark, this is Mr. Pokallas. I was wondering when you might need a new model for your class…"

"Model? Harold, model for what? What are you doing, Harold? Oh, Baby Jesus, I knew you'd lose your marbles one day, now you're strutting around naked, calling strange men on the telephone, buying the wrong milk…"

Dennis Wornick

SILENT-FILM STARLET

Sayre Quevedo

From above, the Rose is a swell of lines, a topographical tracing of petals and pollen. Its stem, depending, may be broad, jagged or, if domesticated, a thin naked thing.

He sets the mirror by the bed
so he can watch himself
make love to her, the silent-film starlet.

She is the unlucky one,
dressed like a wedding.

The rose is a living thing, with fibers to lace it together. The petals of some particular roses are the pigment of tissues used to dam bleeding noses.

He runs his hands over her hips,

against the plump of her thighs.

The starlet stumbles to the terrace,

she mouths the names of the bastard sons

that she will birth him,

collapsing into a sea-foam armchair

she awakes.

Roses laid on graves, thrown at weddings. Planted in gardens. Petals strewn about on bed-sheets, and cakes. Worn behind ears and between teeth. The rose is a livid, many-faceted thing.

Nile Washington

PARENTAL POEM

Vivian Ponte-Fritz

Father tip off the day, hat up, sun never hitting the light eyes
of a gentle, caringman
The only one
The biggest regret for the mother, constant disappointment.
Constant disappearance. No weight is lifted off shoulders,
the load gets bigger and we all begin to slouch.
Not quite grouch or villain: pops advice not pills, in-
-ternal visions blurred, glasses never on, can't seem to find
prescription or perspective.
His position is reflected, magnetized by those that spring off
the tumbling wall of mommy and daddy, the parental cliff.
To take cliff notes would leave a cliff hanger. Because
nobody runs, it doesn't seem to matter, the conversations
scatter beyond reason or maturity.
Yelling through silent treatments: what is left unsaid. At this
time of year, the cat goes unfed. At this time of year, home
is a place of dread. Nothing is quite dead
yet all is ghostly small and understated and all is contem-
plated. No one can
fly or laugh or dance.
The only one
Doesn't wear the pants

Daniella Kessel

Natalie Bigelow

Early morning, still dark
Three boatloads of girls in layers
Wheeling boats down to the water –
creak, scrape, splash.
They talk incessantly, and complain
We don't win our races.

ON FEET AND SHOES

Kanti Keislar

1

~ *13 years ago.*

It's late morning on a bright sunny day. I'm walking into Payless Shoe Source holding Papa's hand.

My first day of pre-school is coming up and I need a new pair of shoes. Together, Papa and I walk down the aisle of shoes for young girls and stop at a small raised platform with foot-shaped cutouts of each shoe size carried in the store. I slip off my right shoe and put my little four-year old foot on the first cutout. Too small. I put my foot on the next one. Better, but still a bit too small. My foot fits into the third cutout. We check the number on the bottom of the cutout, then find the section of the aisle that has shoes in my size.

A minute later, Papa pulls a box from a shelf and shows them to me. The shoes are light brown sandals with Velcro straps. On the straps are Megara, a lady with a Roman-style purple dress and big brown hair, and Pegasus, a white winged horse with a blue mane and tail. I recognize them from the Hercules movie Papa took me to see not too long ago. He helps me put them on and I walk up the aisle, look-ing down at the most beautiful, perfect shoes in the world. I want to wear them out of the store, but I also want to carry the shoebox. Since I'll be wearing the shoes for the rest of my life, I settle on leaving them in the box and carrying it, in a bag, out of the store myself.

Several months later, well assimilated into my morning routine of getting ready for preschool, I realize that my toes are curling over the edge of the sandals and the top. The soft Velcro straps barely reach halfway to the end of the rougher Velcro on the side of the shoes. I'm taken back to Payless to get a new pair of shoes, but for a while I keep the brown sandals on the shoe shelf, where I get to see Megara and Pegasus every morning anyways.

2

Once upon a time in a dream.

Another bright sunny morning.

I'm walking up a big hill. Even though it's slightly rocky, it shouldn't be that hard to climb. But I'm wearing red stilettos. I've never worn stilettos, being just in elementary school, so I'm going very slowly.

My imaginary friend, very real and tangible in this dream, bounces up the hill ahead of me. Her name is Lorna Basky and she's a laundry basket. She's turquoise with yellow handles and there are lots of holes in her sides. She offers me a ride, and I accept.

I climb into my laundry basket friend and she starts bouncing up the hill again. I bounce with her. The pointy heels get stuck in the holes in Lorna's sides and I try to take the shoes off, but it's like my feet are glued into them.

We come to the top of the hill and there's a dragon sitting on the other side, bathing in the sun. She's the same red color as my stilettos. Lorna is too scared to move. I try to urge her back down the other side of the hill, but the dragon has really good ears and hears my whispers. She draws herself up at least 5 stories high, blocking the sun. "YOU STOLE MY SHOES," she bellows.

Lorna and I look down at her feet. She has human feet, tiny compared to her huge body. Glad to relieve myself of the shoes I can't walk in but terrified of the dragon, I attempt again to untangle the stilettos from the holes in Lorna, but can't. The dragon advances as Lorna and I quiver.

I wake up.

3

December 22, 2004.

Overcast, early morning.

Despite having been up past midnight at the hospital waiting for Papa to come out of bypass surgery, I wake up very early. Everyone is still in bed (Shoree in hers and Karan with Mama in the bed she usually shares with Papa) as I shower and dress. My feet are cold. Instead of picking out a pair of socks I walk downstairs to the shoe shelf and find the huge, soft grey slippers Papa wears at home in the house. I can fit both of my feet in a single one of the slippers but I put one in each and go to the kitchen to make breakfast. I awkwardly climb onto the counter, still wearing the slippers, and pull out a box of Malt-O-Meal.

When I get back down onto the floor, I stare at the instructions on the back of the box. I've never made Malt-O-Meal on my own before. Papa, the master Malt-O-Meal maker, has always helped me on the few occasions I've made it.

The banging of measuring cup, heavy pot, and wooden

spoon wake Mama up. She comes downstairs into the kitchen and stands at the door, watching with puffy eyes as I pull a small footstool up the stove. She leaves and several seconds later calls from the hallway, asking if I've seen Papa's slippers. Obviously, she hadn't noticed I was wearing them. I call back to her no, hastily kicking the slippers under a green table nearby. When Mama comes back I have climbed onto the footstool and I'm holding a measuring cup. She watches me as I pour the milk into the pot on the stove. I get off the footstool and walk across the kitchen to the opposite counter, where I'd left the box of Malt-O-Meal mix. She hears the pit-pat of my feet and looks down.

"Aren't your feet cold?"

"No," I reply.

Later she asks me to tell her if I see Papa's slippers. He'd called and asked her to bring a few things to him in the hospital because he'll be there for a couple more days. I eventually put the slippers back on the shoe shelf, where Mama finds them on her way out to visit Papa.

4

Regular canvas Converse shoes don't keep your feet very warm or rainwater out.

5

Summer 2007.

It's yet another late morning, bright and sunny, though considerably warmer.

I'm wearing a brown, beige, and red cotton salwar kameez—loose pants and long tunic, with a dupata, or scarf. My mother, my sister, a family friend and I are setting out on a day-long pilgrimage of sorts, to walk to the goshala (an Indian cow shelter), the Jamuna River, and several temples and holy locations in Vrndavana.

We each hold our japa bead bags with our right hands, because it's considered disrespectful to say your japa prayers while holding the bead bag in your left hand. In our left hands we carry our Old Navy flip-flops. The ground beneath us changes from dirt to gravel to sand to dirt again, now a little muddier.

I know we're arriving at the goshala because cows are wandering slowly down the path in both directions. As we pass them we run our hands along them and ask for their blessings. I look down at their scratched, muddy hooves and wonder how much they feel through them. We arrive at the goshala and put our shoes back on. The workers walk around among the cows barefoot, only sometimes putting on wooden or plastic shoes when they enter the pens. Down along the Jamuna River, almost nobody is wearing shoes – the people visiting the holy locations and temples, the man selling soda in glass bottles, and the little kids who shriek as they chase goats, pigs, and more wandering cows.

I look down at my own feet. The pedicure my adopted cousins gave me in Pakistan last week will be gone by the end of the day.

CALLING ALL TEEN WRITERS AND ARTISTS!

To submit your work for publication in this winter's Anthology,
send it to teenswrite2010@gmail.com by October 15th, 2010.

Made in the USA
Charleston, SC
26 May 2010